BORDERLAND ROADS

BORDERLAND ROADS:

SELECTED POEMS OF HŎ KYUN

Translated by

IAN HAIGHT AND T'AE-YŎNG HŎ

WHITE PINE PRESS / BUFFALO, NEW YORK

Translators' Note: Romanization of Chinese proper names follows the Pinyin system, as translated at www.mandarintools.com. Romanization of Korean proper names follows the McCune-Reischauer system, as translated at www.romanization.org.

Publication of this book was made possible, in part, with public funds from the New York State Council on the Arts, a State Agency, and by grants from the Deasan Foundation and the Sunshik Min Endowment for the Advancement of Korean Literature at the Korea Institute, Harvard University.

Acknowledgments:
"Longing for Hwang County Women" was first published in *Portland Review*
"Crossing Iron Mountain River" was first published in *Asheville Poetry Review*
"Saying Goodbye to Ryu, Yŏn-suk" was first published in *Circumference.*
"Intimate Pain," "Sending Away a Visitor," and "Writing" were first published in *Spoon River Poetry Review.*

Cover Art: "About Sunset" (2002) by Ch'un Jŏn appears courtesy of Chŏng-ŭn Kim.

First Edition.

ISBN: 978-1-935210-08-5

Printed and bound in the United States of America.

Library of Congress Control Number: 2009932983

WHITE PINE PRESS
P.O. BOX 236
BUFFALO, NEW YORK 14201
www.whitepine.org

Thank you, Beatrix Gates and Ann Michael, for writing wisdom.

Contents

Timeline of Events / 9

Introduction / 13

WAR AND OCCUPATION

At the Refugee Camp, I Write Eight Poems / 21
After Du Fu's "Old Memories" Poems, I / 23
Over-nighting in a Country House / 24
Upon Arrival in Kangnŭng / 26
July 7th, Evening, Reciting a Mournful Poem / 27
After Du Fu's "Old Memories" Poems, II / 28
Writing What I See / 30
After Du Fu's "Old Memories" Poems, III / 32
Poems in Short Form / 34
Saying Goodbye to Ryu, Yŏn-suk / 38
Climbing to "Wide View" Pavilion / 39
Visiting King Guan's Tomb in Northern China / 40
During the Full Moon: a Response to a Poem / 41

LIFE AFTER WAR

Crossing Iron Mountain River / 45
On the Way / 46
Written on the Ferry at Peaceful River / 47
Sharing Poems: My Word is "Mountain" / 48
The Longing of Hwang County Women / 49
A Small Peach / 51
Intimate Pain / 52
Lamenting the Self / 53
Early Morning, Leaving Seoul's Last Hamlets / 54
Writing / 55

Going Out to the Fields / 56
A Small Gathering at "Pristine" Pavilion / 57
A Displaced Widow's Resentment / 58
The Valley of 10,000 Waterfalls / 60
Tosol Temple / 61
Arriving at the County Office / 62
Indulgence / 63
Lazy Old Man Visits / 64
On Being Passed Over for an Appointment / 65
Self Misery / 66
Falling Blossoms / 67
First Feelings on Arriving at Samch'ŏk County / 69
Writing in My Study / 70
Upon Hearing of My Dismissal / 71
An Improvised Poem / 72
A Forest of Fragrant Flowers / 73
Remorse / 74
Waiting on Judgment in Prison / 75
Recalling Happiness / 76
Writing Sorrow II / 77
Sending Away a Visitor, Sitting Alone / 78
Ending a Collection / 79

Endnotes / 80

Appendix 1: Lands and Locations / 86

Appendix 2: Reference for Important Names / 88

Appendix 3: Excerpts from 2006 Text / 91

Bibliography / 94

About the Translators / 99

TIMELINE OF EVENTS

1569: Hŏ Kyun is born.

1583-5: Pong, Kyun's elder brother, is exiled for three years because he will not compromise with the King on matters of courtly politics. Kyun probably loved and admired Pong most among all his brothers.

1588: Pong dies.

1589: Kyun and a friend, Yi, I-ch'ŏm, pass their first state exams together. Nansŏrhŏn, Kyun's elder sister, dies.

1592: April 14, Japan invades Korea. Approximately two weeks after the invasion, Seoul is captured.
—July 7th, Kyun's wife delivers their first son.
—July 10th, Kyun's wife dies.
—A few days after the death of his wife, Kyun's son dies. The exact date is unknown.

1593: Kyun spends the year in retreat at his hometown in Kangnŭng. He rebuilds his grandfather's house, the house he was born in. He spends most of his time at this house and Naksan Temple.

1594: Kyun passes the second state exams for promotion and is sent on his first diplomatic mission to China. Upon his return he is eligible for another promotion, but when his mother dies, he goes to Kangnŭng.

1595: According to custom, Kyun is supposed to spend three years in reserved mourning while residing in a hovel next to his mother's grave, but flaunts the tradition by openly carousing with courtesans. His unapologetic attitude earns him his first significant political notoriety.

1596: Kyun returns to Seoul and is given charge of all diplomatic documents.

1597: March of this year, Kyun briefly becomes tutor to the Crown Prince.

—April of this year, Kyun earns the highest marks on the state promotion exams. He is sent to China to request help in removing the Japanese forces from Korea. Later in the year major hostilities erupt between the Chinese and Japanese armies in Korea.

—October of this year Kyun is transferred at the same grade to the Defense Ministry. His duties are to serve, attend to, and entertain the Chinese diplomats and generals in Korea.

1598: The Japanese army retreats from the peninsula when the Shogun, Toyotomi Hideyoshi, dies. Kyun and a Chinese poet together edit a collection of Korean poetry. The collection includes poems by Kyun's sister, Nansŏrhŏn.

1599-1609: These years for Kyun are fraught with long periods of diplomatic service abroad and short periods of domestic appointments. Kyun goes abroad so frequently because of his lack of manners. His forthrightness earns him not only notoriety, but political enemies.

1610-11: While in exile, Kyun edits his entire works to date.

1612: Kyun's elder brother Sŏng dies, and with him, Kyun's last familial ally in the government. This is also the year Kyun writes his famous novel, *Hong, Kil-tong*, meant to enlighten lower classes. A classic of Korean literature, it is the first novel written in Korean.

1613: Political unrest begins when seven sons of concubines ask the king for equal political and social opportunity. Eventually the men are executed. Kyun likely played a role in organizing and helping the men, but any participation he may have had in this event goes undiscovered.

1615: Kyun becomes a minister through the help of his treacherous friend, Yi, I-ch'ŏm.

1618: Kyun is drawn and quartered on charges of treason, charges drawn up by I-ch'ŏm as part of a purge to eliminate his political enemies.

2006: A new collection of 382 poems by Kyun is discovered, mostly centered on personal and courtly life, traveling to China, and life in China. The collection covers the period August, 1615 to March, 1616.

Hŏ Kyun: An Interpretive Introduction

You don't want to leave Seoul, but you have to. When your brother, the Vice Ambassador, returned from Japan, you'd heard. The King, on the advice of others, however, decided invasion was unlikely. Hundreds of years of peace, a close ally in China, and a belief in the inferiority of the "island barbarians" led him to think Japan would not act. The army did not prepare any contingency plans for war, and most generals did not give war a second thought.

They were wrong. A week ago the Japanese landed in Pusan. Your country's armies possess few guns, are outnumbered, and unlike the invaders, haven't fought a war for generations. The commanders now seem more concerned about running off with their concubines and treasuries of cities. Only a few defend their posts, mostly lower officers, and they are quickly defeated. When your generals do possess a strategic or tactical advantage, they still run like cowards at the first signs of serious engagement.

"What choice does the King have?" you ask. "What choice does anyone have under circumstances such as these?" The long line of nobles and citizens leaving Seoul is pelted by garbage and stones. Promises to defend the city are empty. After two days, the city burns, not from the Japanese, but slaves destroying their government records of ownership. It is not just that you understand why the slaves do this, but that you empathize with them. Of course, this is a secret you tell no one.

Two months pass. There are other secrets—anguishes—you want to tell but won't. Your wife is pregnant, due any day in a relentless midsummer heat. You have a mule for her, but she shouldn't be moving this much, certainly not in this heat. You have food and water, but you must be careful with it. The roads are full, there is no place to sleep. Everywhere there are people in retreat. Your entourage of servants is a help, but there is only so much they can do when everyone is desperate and resources are scarce.

When your wife enters labor, shelter becomes a farmer's shanty that smells of cow dung and urine. Her servants know midwifery, but the birth is not easy. Your wife bleeds and they cannot stop it. The village stream water looks like it might not be safe, even after boiling. People continue to pass by on the nearby road. The heat doesn't end.

Your wife dies. There is little time to mourn, barely enough time for burial. The Japanese, so you have heard, may be near. You must continue moving. Your first son—there is some joy in that.

Is it the heat that makes your son cry? Or does he know the fact his mother is dead? He wants milk, but there is none. He is too young for rice; even rice gruel is too much for his tender stomach. The servant women cannot swaddle his head and neck for travel safely because he is newly-born. Perhaps it is good that he never opens his eyes to this world, does not see the hunger of the common refugee people, their fatigue, their fear, their collapsing by the roadside in despair and resignation. He no longer cries at night, just three days after the passing of your wife.

You have no time to mourn the loss of your son. Often babies do not live their first hundred days under normal circumstances. For now, there can be nothing to regret. There is only to press on, in the name of your country, King, and family, if nothing else.

You travel overland through rugged mountains that the enemy will likely never approach. Beautiful as this land is, few want to live here, except recluses and hermits. There is an unforgettable tranquility to this land of waterfalls, valley ridges, and forests—a peacefulness that resides in the heart of your country's people. It reminds you of home, and gives you purpose; there is somewhere to go. When you arrive on the eastern shores of your country, you sail south; and finally you reach your destination: your hometown, Kangnŭng.

The enemy will not come here. You are sure of that. It requires traversing dense mountains with narrow paths, the only way to get to where you are—a place of no military value to the enemy. What would they gain by coming to Kangnŭng? A large freshwater lake beside the ocean's tourmaline-blue waters. A high hilltop pavilion looking out over fields of rice, the lake, and the ocean. There are the five full moons: the one in the sky, the one reflected on the lake, another on the ocean, and in your cup of wine, and best of all, the one in your lover's eyes. After all you have suffered, love is what you most crave, and you take it passionately when you can find it.

You desire not only love. Your family has a name and a tradition. There is something to live up to, including intellectual self-respect. The Japanese burned your library, but they did not, could not, kill you. And maybe, finally, life's purposes are simply human. *We must not forget what it means to be human. We must not forget our cultural sensibilities.* And so you study Du Fu, among others, as your father, his friends, your brothers, and your sister did. You write a book at the age of twenty-five: *Comments on Contemporary Criticism.* You write it mostly from what you remember of your library, and the few resources you can find in your family houses. For you the book is not merely a scholarly exercise: it is an act of preservation, a demonstration of prowess in dire circumstances; it is an act of defiance against time.

You hear the King is alive and the main Japanese army has halted near P'yŏngyang. There is talk of the Chinese sending an army to defend Korea. "Where," the King wonders, "have all the court officials gone when now they are most desperately needed?" Filled with purpose, you pass the government exams for promotion and are sent on your first diplomatic mission to China. You impress the Chinese with your knowledge of their history, culture, language, and literature. Occasionally you hear the diplomats whisper, "How can he know more about Wang Can than we do?" And you know about the moon, about courtesans, their songs, and maybe most important of all, wine.

The Chinese grow even more sympathetic to Korea due to your efforts. After your service period is over, you return to work for the Korean court directly, but your mother dies, and so you return to Kangnŭng. Is it success? Is it power? Or is it simply you possess the creative, passionate individualism of genius? You find reasons for publicly breaking rules when you could do so privately without punishment. Where is the line that divides calculated martyrdom and hubris, the line between acting with a lack of foresight, and, one might even say, stupidity? You tell men about your "ranking book" for courtesans when you should, by all appearances, be mourning your mother. Where is your discretion? When tutoring the Crown Prince, you insist he learn Tang poets instead of the traditional Song so that he might write with plain but astute precision—your chosen style. Worst of all, you question the Prince's intelligence when he fails to memorize his lessons.

The King, however, cannot disregard your talents. When you pass the government exams for promotion (has it been four times with full marks?), you become Deputy Vice Minister of Foreign Affairs, charged with the special purpose of handling the diplomacy of Chinese military support against Japan. Through your duties, you are introduced to prominent Chinese literati. You edit your first collection of poems—poems that you can remember, lost in the war; others salvaged from notes. Your poems become the only ones in Korean literature about the war with Japan. You introduce the Chinese to your sister Nansŏrhŏn's poetry. They admire the craft—astonishingly, better than Li Bai. One might even call her talent supernatural. They revere her as a Taoist Immortal. Because of demand for copies of her poems, the paper stores in the capital run out of paper. It will be years, though, before the literary establishment in Korea, her own country, accepts her as the greatest female poet in Korean literature.

The Japanese eventually leave the Korean peninsula. For them, it has been years of extended supply lines, harrassment by the small but surprisingly superior Korean navy, and the ever-present indefatigable Chinese army. The dues of occupying a hostile country have taken a heavy toll. When the Japanese Shogun dies, the new leader ends the war.

Years pass. The King has not forgotten your accomplishments, talents, and intelligence, but you don't follow courtly or political decorum. You speak your mind. Maybe you are right to do so. Maybe you are wrong. The results are clear enough: you get sent abroad on diplomatic missions extraordinarily frequently. When you return home, your government service periods are short. It's impossible to earn much money for your family under circumstances such as these. Your children and wife suffer. Some days, your family, though from a lineage of nobles who have served King and country with distinction, has no food.

What is it that sustains you? Why is it so hard to follow the old ways? You remember an elder brother's sharp tongue, how he spoke out against the King's anti-Confucianism, how, *he said*, the King was hurting the Royal Family. You haven't forgotten the result: endless exiles, poor health, misery, and finally death. This is the price one pays for being right; you accept what being right costs.

There is so much wrong. Why is it intelligent, talented, passionate women (like your sister) have no public place in Korean life except as professional courtesans? Why must the sons of concubines (like your beloved teacher and friend, Yi Tal)—no matter how smart, no matter how wise— be prevented from any meaningful government position? Why are people executed for questioning the King's law, even though according to the law, they have the right to question? Why should the poor pay rice taxes when they cannot feed themselves, and the county treasuries overflow with grain? Your list, like the suffering of the people, has no end.

You find your friends among the disenfranchised: the sons of concubines, the literati who have lost power or never had political connections, or those who, like you, are tired of the system and want no part of it. You write simple, plain-spoken poems that avoid the traditional aesthetics of the upper class, disavowing their literary embellishments. You write about the poor, about writing, about political life at court—how you wish it would end. You believe literature should be available to common people, and so you begin to eschew writing in the traditional Chinese for the Korean vernacular. You write a novel—what we today might call a "Robin Hood" adventure—about a man who governs an island off the coast of Korea. The island nation is still loyal to Korea and its King, but is governed by a separate system of laws, allowing more opportunity for women, those who are not of noble class, and the poor. None of this escapes the notice of King and court. Some mark your days as numbered.

Your father and elder brothers have all died. You are the oldest male in your family, and it is your duty to help your family's next generation find a successful place in government service. You realize that if you want Korea to change, to be more open to common people and their needs, you will have to have some position of power. You choose an influential man to help, one who once was a sincere friend: Yi, I-ch'ŏm. Years of political life have disintegrated Yi's moral fiber, and he is now a treacherous man who only seeks to use you. However, you do become a Minister through Yi's help, and so you trust what he says.

It's another dispute at court: the King wants his stepmother, the Queen Mother, out of the palace because he hates her. You think the King has the right to throw her out, while others don't. Rumors fly, charges are made, punishments are meted out among the factions. The King has his way, but the losers haven't forgotten the winners, and wait to exact their vengeance. You become a ripe target for your enemies, those who seek to abuse your trust and those who want to use you to purge their enemies.. You are charged with treason. You think how you never should have written that book about the separate island from Korea. Yi, I-ch'ŏm, the man whom you trust, the friend who made you Minister, explains to you how you will be vindicated. You believe him and so make no defense to the King. The King does not understand the details of the charges, and he wants to hear from you. But your friend, I-ch'ŏm, is lying to him too. Yi tells the King your silence is an admission of guilt. What can he do? The King reluctantly orders the death sentence to be carried out.

You have several thoughts before this story, this life, ends. There is so much to consider and reflect upon. There is the confusion about the treachery, or maybe you think Yi simply failed in his mission to defend you. The evidence was too overpowering for the King to ignore. It is fated for you to die now. Was it wrong to fight for the lives of others? How many more years would you have gained by doing nothing? How many works went unwritten? What could have been different had you been more respectful in your tone?

The oxen pulled hard. It was a slow rending of your limbs from your body. You deserved better than that.

Other matters of the sentencing were failures. Yes, your house was torn down and burned. Yes, what writings of yours that could be found were put to the torch. Your genius and your love of people, though, were unforgettable. Maybe the King secretly had a few books—the important ones—"misplaced" in the royal library. Even if he didn't, your words had touched the nation. People refused to forget you. And now, almost four hundred years later, in a different language, you are remembered again.

—Ian Haight and T'ae-yŏng Hŏ,
Summer, 2009

War and Occupation

At the Refugee Camp

I

My home is in Changnung, east of a small market—
a thatched house with several small rooms, now empty.
So many of my scrolls were cataloged, but where are they now?
Perhaps thrown in a ditch, or buried under earth.

II

A few days ago, when court meetings adjourned, the wide street
filled with the *jingle* of waist pendants; ten thousand houses bubbled
      with courtesans
and fluttering flutes. Now the King has left his palace—the field for
      singing and dancing
has become a battleground.

III

My father's grave is on the banks of the Han River.
At year's end, who will tend his tomb?
I look west to the pine trees, heartbroken—the sun sets
at the sky's edge—my handkerchief, wet with tears.

IV

The road's endless distance to West Castle's river border—
since leaving, it is difficult to send letters. I see only spears.
My refugee life, entrusted to others,
where will I enjoy clouds—spend a day in leisurely sleep?

V

Near the northern border, enemy swords still have not been broken.
When will the greedy pigs leave the central kingdom?
At day's end, beacon-post fires have all been quelled.
I sit, knowing the enemy will not confront this battle-ready mountain.

VI

A thousand foot castle wall surrounded by a hundred foot ditch—
the soldiers wield sharp arrows, strong bows, and long swords.
Clappers sound in front of the castle tents; soldiers speak with one
        another:
"Our governor will surely be defeated."

VII

At every station in my life, I've liked to act as a simple sick monk:
during hushed nights in my thatched house, I sit, facing a hooded candle.
It is difficult to melt away old habits of my luxurious life—
tomorrow on the plain, I plan a day of hawking.

VIII

At this river crossing, my friend, in the purple glow of evening, seemed a
        river spirit.
Once he left and letters ended, distance between us grew immense.
I cherish a memory of last year, during a moon like this night's,
when we rode side by side in the snow to fetch tea water.

1597*

After Du Fu's "Old Memories" Poems, I

The King rests not in his palace, but a borderland guesthouse for envoys—
the last general defends Bird Pass.
I only see an urgent letter from a retreating northern army—
I still have not heard of victory from the south.

Sun sets on the autumn plains; remnants of armies grieve—
a sad wind blows on the Yi River, bringing defeated warriors.
A small joy to see a wise magistrate from Yangyang,
with lance and horse, defending our gate.

1597*

Over-nighting in a Country House

I

Outside the castle, a somber flute
sounds through dead silence of night.

Upon a wall, the slanting moon
spreads serious brows.

Far across the flowing river,
a distant enemy castle—

at a seaside village,
our general's flags ripple brightly.

II

Wang Can slumped in his pavilion,
wrote poems in vain.

Du Fu had no posting,
so could only write poems.

People say the blood of war
floods all rivers.

What person can devise a plan
to drive away the enemy?

III

Below the moon's radiance, a lingering fog clears,
releasing a mountain—

male servants converse
about tomorrow morning's travels.

I continue the dance of my escape, but you, my companion, stop.
You think my lack of rest strange.

Though absurd roosters may crow in daylight,
it doesn't mean they'll have bad luck.

1592

Upon Arrival in Kangnŭng

On the East Sea, wind blew our sails open—
after 1,000 li and nine days
we've come to Kangnŭng.

A playful dragon holds a flaming marble, jumps into the Po Sea—
a crane gleefully carries a beaming ruby in its mouth
as it flies from the Mountain of Immortals.

Through the chop of waves, Han envoys once came to Korea.
The Qin Emperor commanded like a stone-tipped whip,
and his envoys came as well, despite the windy rain—
they sought an Immortality elixir.

After dying 10,000 deaths, a soul finally can rest.
The cycles of life are so ridiculous to me!

1592

July 7th, Evening, Reciting a Mournful Poem

On this day last year,
I was a desperate refugee.
Swathed in silk,
my first precious son
was born.

Who knows Anren's grief,
how he mourned his wife,
or Zi Xia's sorrow, blind
from the loss of his son,
and how he left Confucius?

In one short year
people's lives change
to pain.
I suffer a sickness:

late at night
I doubly-feel
the loss of joy—

lifting my eyes to Vega,
our tears rain down.

1593

After Du Fu's "Old Memories" Poems, II

I

Hilts of double dragons roar at night,
blades longing to be drawn.

In this desperate moment,
my voice is lessened—

it's impossible to be the King's counsel.
I once wrote on a pillar

my impassioned devotion to country—
though I work hard

I cannot do as much as Zhuge.
I recline in a pavilion now

my hair gray—
my writings pale in comparison to Zuo Si.

I'm well-prepared for my trip
to the King's western fortresses—

please don't doubt
my finding a brilliant tactician.

II

An old man kneels in his yard,
an officer shouts at the gate—

I remember
Du Fu's Shihao Village.

At the government office,
the time to collect taxes nears—

an old wife cries, starving,
her eyes already dull.

She tries to gather iron,
but finds only a small lump—

less lucky, drafted soldiers,
killed, become lone ghosts.

Collecting taxes doesn't end
people's suffering—

how can I describe the sorrow
my eyes have seen?

1597

Writing What I See

I

An old wife sits at dusk, grieving
in her charred village.

Her unkempt hair, like frost—
both eyes, muted.

Her husband imprisoned
by creditors.

Her son, drafted, follows the King's son,
bound for Ch'ŏngju.

In a house assaulted by war,
pillars and beams burn.

The daily work can't be done—
her will to live has ceased.

I hide in a mountain forest
without my hemp dress shirt.

What business remains for an officer,
calling at the gates?

II

Two old men
who're not unhappy

talk about how smart
this year's governor is:

"He's captured stray Japanese horses,
feeds them at his house."

"He keeps the army provisions
in storehouses by the sea."

Charred remains of thatched houses
give people no shelter,

but to dig the castle's moat,
half a family is called away.

People say all the King's soldiers
march to Sangwŏn—

who then will defend this castle
as well as General Suiyang?

1597*

After Du Fu's "Old Memories" Poems, III

I

Last night, Chinese soldiers
crossed the wide Yalu River

into Korea—
at dawn, bardered cavalry

galloped with unfurled flags.
Strong bows, strung and tested,

pulled to the shape of a moon—
sparkling swords, ready to cut hairs

placed on their edges.
The Chinese soldiers have built ramparts—

their flutes and drums
anticipate a general's jubilant victory.

All Koreans delight in the Emperor's grace for our tears,
though he wearies of our praises.

II

On a high plateau, night ends,
as it did in General Tiahou's calm and confident camp—

like Han Emperors of old,
we have long arrows

eager to *swish*
through autumn air.

Outside our castle, scaling ladders and rams
fill a hundred roads

toward enemy camps—
drums and horns

of a thousand squads
sound from our trenches.

The border magistrate
adheres to Yellow Stone's strategies—

the generals learned their sword craft
from the legendary White Monkey.

Returning on their saddles, they'll drink blood,
heads hanging from their banners—

the business of heroes, old and new,
remains the same.

1597*

Poems in Short Form

I

In Snow Pear House
silk curtains drape low—

the sun draws down
below picturesque balustrades.

No one walks
to my quiet country home—

only a ringdove's full-throated cry
fills the air.

II

I depart a Buddhist temple
with my ten small trunks of books—

spending March in Myŏngju,
I find my sideburns spotted gray.

I cannot leave for Seoul
until the sweetbriar petals have all fallen—

when night comes, I dream again
of courtly service.

III

The talents of Hongnong
write plentifully and with splendor—

they are violet stars
in a clear sky above fertile fields.

Those writers enjoy facing west wind through their windows,
wishing their intoxicated dreams would come true

just as Li Bai's great brush
blossomed to a rose.

IV

Poets live in Tanyang
and study Dongpo.

They pour a galaxy of words onto paper—
towns celebrate their poems.

Please, do not live as Du Fu,
thin and sickly in old age—

rather live within the palace gates
and write a river of silver.

V

Early in my life, I learned
the difficult Tang poems—

when writing, my poems
were better than Yin Keng and He Xun.

Who knew in late fall
among the West River Poets

which would not catch a whale
among the blue sea's waves?

VI

Kim, Chong-chik was a worthy poet, like Du Fu.
One hundred years of persecution,

even after death, consumes his reputation
as an overgrown valley path.

His remaining writings, a perfume—
even now, they seem everlasting.

Great poems—bejewelled pendants of jade—
I'm unable to write.

VII

Yi Tal read poems
until his hair turned gray.

He wrote so many poems,
all worthy of Liu, Zhangqing.

Now, even if people's coarse eyes
only mock

he won't be forgotten
in the wide river of time, endlessly coursing.

VIII

A friend went north,
wanting a poem to be written for his painting—

having failed, he returned home,
his head full of wine.

Naturally, he visited Pear Blossom Pavilion
in the moonlight. Perhaps, looking at the sea

through an upturned glass, he accepted
that for him, it would only be a small pond.

1597*

Saying Goodbye to Ryu, Yŏn-suk

Wearing traveling clothes,
like a small quail, alone—
in your bags, the timid
cither
in your kist, books.

People say you have the craziness of Li Bai
but our old friends
think of you as sickly Xiangru.

Wind turns on the curved pond,
cools the pavilion railings—
sunlight spreads a dark shade of light
on my silk-curtained window.

In Seoul, if anyone asks about me,
tell them I've left life
for the paradise of fishing.

1597*

Climbing to "Wide View" Pavilion

The high pavilion leans into strong wind—
I climb slowly to this secluded hilltop.
Though there's war
something of value remains to observe:
this morning, I began a poem about the view.
After cleansing rain, the blue mountains seem nearer—
fog drifts in far away green fields.
Like a feather, fatigue from long travel passes—
the western sun sinks under arches of a bridge.

1597

Visiting King Guan's Tomb in Northern China

At the front gate, a moss-covered gravestone:
wind from a forest blows to this shrine.

At the corner of a building, a banner—
a shed, glossed in evening sun.

By the wall, cedars and firs
rustle in wind. Roof beams

of faded willow-leaf red and bud blue—
your picture endures clouds and thunder.

I burn incense for the ghosts in this place,
but not paper money—it invites resentful spirits.

A night cuckoo cries, as if spitting blood—
the blood, reddening zinnia petals.

1597

During the Full Moon: a Response to a Poem

I

The order of seasons belongs now to mid-autumn—
a year lasts fleetingly.
I enjoy poems endearing the moon—
the skill and emotion, a matchless pearl.

II

The perfect mid-autumn—
golden waves flood the sky.
Late at night, I lean into pure light:
the clear scenery, aglow this time of year.

III

A lustrous white galaxy—
cold radiance ripples from Heaven's Jade City.
Moon nymphs seem to speak to me
in this new phase of illumination.

IV

Strolling my garden, the pull of shadows—
rays of cold penetrate bones of men.
I want to speak with Li Bai—
raising a wineglass, I address the moon.

V

Facing this landscape, I want to sip wine—
sadness rends this traveler's heart.
Since times of old, men have looked to the moon—
who can endure as this light has?

VI

My country also has a bright moon—
my family's sorrow, from desolate solitude.
It's natural to pity me, a stranger over 10,000 li away—
together, at the sky's shores, we pass through night.

VII

A young courtesan from Beili plucks strings—
guests sing at an eastern neighbor's house.
This treasure of moonlight—
for whom does it shine?

1597

Life After War

Crossing Iron Mountain River

Sunset. I arrive
at an old ferry.
A west wind blows—
alone, I cross.
Dark waves rush south,
the north, plentiful
with new autumn colors.
The year goes—
I've already said it all.
How are the gardens at home?
In mid-flow, the sudden grief
of disappointment—
on the river, songs
of fishermen drift.

1598

On the Way

Sweet-scented, cloud-shrouded mountains—
far from my home,
I cannot return.
Three years of government service
have buried me in horse dust.

Going south
then a trip to the north—
late autumn has already come.

I cannot bear
this, another sunset
across Iron Mountain River.

1598

Written on the Ferry at Peaceful River

My horse and I float across the widespread river—
I hear a workingman's heartsick song.

The river sounds swift in autumn—
though it's late season, trees bear many leaves.

From the forest river bend, sails pass south—
before frost, borderland geese fly overhead.

This year, I'm riding an envoy's horse again,
but I will never regret my missteps.

1598

Sharing Poems: My Word is "Mountain"

I bore a hard illness, lying sick for ten days—
snow piles buried my brushwood door.
Where did these old poets come from,
cheering my weary face?
I raise a lantern, sitting in my warm room;
we face each other in our white hats.
Si-mang is a simple, informal drinker,
O-jŏng is calm and easy-going.
Forgetting our circumstances in endless laughter,
the melodious evening
lasts beyond the peace of midnight.
Smooth wine is better than fresh raw fish—
women with soft braided hair sing delicate songs.
We forget how far we have traveled—
everywhere here feels like Seoul.

Stars fall into light; the galaxy's river turns.
A new moon pales into endless blue—
the pleasure ends. *I must feel no pain of parting.*
My life has had endless troubles—
a man lives merely a hundred years.
Over time, it grows difficult to pull a carriage swiftly—
how long will duties shape my life?
Leaving the grime of politics,
I have a plan to retire—
soon I will stroll my village, and the spring-like,
vine-covered east mountain.

1599

The Longing of Hwang County Women

I

Before me lies Perfect Direction Mountain,
below, Full-Silk Valley.
It's better to live in a brothel
than marry a peddler.

II

My peddler sails on a river. He promised to return by August.
The ninth of September has already passed
the wine has ripened—
why is he late?

III

Women, lovely as flowers, indulge in afternoon naps—
others, graceful as cranes, rendezvous through the night.
The women of day and night seize every moment—
competing with these beauties, how will I find my love?

IV

I love my lotus-layered petals,
but my husband desires another flower.
Rather than visit a park for lovers,
I walk a simple stream for passersby.

V

At night I climb to Great Emptiness Pavilion
to secretly meet a handsome man,
but a clerk official appears,
demanding, "Who is it you are meeting?"

VI

Chengdu has luxuriously smooth silk
with butterflies shimmering among flowers.
For a fee, I slept with a prize—
now I can sew a dress for dancing.

1599

A Small Peach

This February, Changan feels no spring
but by the wall
a new peach
flirtatiously lovely
makes this old poet smile,
like meeting an old friend
at the sky's horizon.

1600

Intimate Pain

I

Fame is not my friend. Only books and history
are close to me. Mountain streams
await my escape—at the ferry crossing,
a dear old friend expects me.

The dangers of government service have grayed my hair—
affairs of family drift like pathetic clouds.
My only power is writing of home,
of mountains, and fragrant spring grass.

II

When do tired birds gather in their nests?
This lonely cloud cannot return home.
The vagueness of fame grays one's hair—
I have a plan—only—to return to Blue Mountain.

Days pass as easily as sitting on a divan—
I enter the simplicity of the world.
A new poem should not be tied to rules of rhyme—
and so my weary face relaxes.

1600

Lamenting the Self

I, an official for the Board of Rites,
am essentially an idiot.
Thirty-two years old,
my hair's already white.
I still hate the arrogance of Anren,
who groveled for power in carriage dust,
and envy Xie Shang's wisdom,
his wearing of the Governor's silk and seal.

So many posts for other men—
these days, I often hear the Prime Minister's scolding.
I want to go to the Mountain of Immortals,
to hear the flute of a crane rider—
but the Queen of Heaven
has not yet called me away.

I know all the prominent faces in Seoul—
their red palace gates, so high
I cannot meet them.
To apply and beg
for a Governor's position
is like climbing to Heaven—
for three-thousand li
before Heaven
there are no clear shallows to cross.

1600

Early Morning, Leaving Seoul's Last Hamlets

The morning driver hurries to depart, ringing a dawn bell—
from the bridge's unwinding road, dense fog descends.
Spring colors silently return to willow banks—
before my horse, the wheel of sun rises over mountains.

Through a life of writing, the early talent recedes—
earning position to change the world—this, my old desire, dies.
Soon I will retire to the country
not caring if others call me a tavern servant.

1601

Writing

A shop's light darkens—
the time for curfew nears.

Riding a horse, wide awake,
I return home in the night.

The Big Dipper slowly moves—
a galaxy dims into daylight.

As the moon remains bright,
I long for the Mountain of Immortals.

Lone bamboo flowers blossom
along the western deck railings.

Wind stirs silk blinds
beneath a beam.

Dawn advances. The moon's milky iridescence—
I play my iron flute.

Outside my sea-blue window,
did I hear a lively phoenix cry?

1602

Going Out to the Fields

Autumn gathers in the ripe fields—
everywhere, there is laughter.

In home after home, people tilt back cups of rice wine—
field after field, dotted with bent yellow stalks of harvest.

It's ridiculous for me to have no fields,
shamefully writing, begging for rice.

In east Seoul, on my three rented ridges,
when will I plow for weeding?

1602

A Small Gathering at "Pristine" Pavilion

December's end bears bitter cold—
again, through the night, my candle slowly weakens.
Fine wine brings us heartfelt songs—
fragrances float through air
as she removes her silks.

So much poverty and illness in the world—
the more my name spreads, the more I am praised and cursed.
This evening, I enjoy conversation—
the year's too-fast passing.

1602

A Displaced Widow's Resentment

West of Ch'ŏrwŏn Castle, the cold sun grays. Evening clouds obscure Pogae Mountain's peak. There, a white-haired widow wears ragged clothes; welcoming this traveler, she leaves her house, opens her brushwood door for me.

"I am an old woman originally from Seoul. When Seoul surrendered to the Japanese soldiers, I left the city with my one son, following my husband. My family's luck had left—we were penniless. We drifted to a different city, depending on the new strange land.

"My feet blistered heavily, so we rested often, hiding in valleys. At night we begged for food; in daylight, we lay concealed. My husband's mother grew sick, so he walked, carrying her on his back. Wandering the steep mountains, there was no time to rest. Rain fell. The black of night thickened. Slipping in puddles, my legs grew tired; I couldn't see my own steps.

"Two robbers had been following us. Their swords drawn, they suddenly sprang from the darkness—both looked so fierce. Their angry swords cut my husband's neck. His mother's face was torn. A son and mother killed— their poor reproaching blood overflowed. I held my young child and ran deep into a forest. The robbers heard him crying, found us, and took him for a slave. I barely escaped the mouth of that tiger; I ran quickly, daring not to speak or make a sound.

"The next morning I went back and found the two corpses. I couldn't tell which was my mother-in-law and which was my husband. Crows and kites pecked at their innards. A dog chewed one of their bones. I cried out for someone to help me move the bodies. I could barely dig a three-foot hole. I gathered and buried what bones I found. Alone, there was no place for my single shadow to go.

"I wandered the forest and found a tavern. The woman of the house felt my sadness; we began to trust each other. She let me pump water and shuck grain for meals. I ate leftover food and wore worn-out clothes. Scorched with despair for twelve years, my face blackened from working in the sun. My hair fell out. My legs and waist stiffened.

"Recently I heard news from Seoul that the robbers kept my son, and by luck, he made it back to Seoul, alive.

"I've heard he became a palace servant, tending cabinets of silk and a full cellar of rice. He took a wife and built a house. Doesn't he miss his mother, or is she still unknown to him, like a stranger in a foreign land?

"My child grew up without any help. Midnight tears have fallen from my cheeks thinking of this.

"My face is wrinkled, and my son already grown—even if we met, would we know each other?

"My old body will fall into a grave, and nothing will be said. Will I ever take my son's wine to his father's tomb?

"I hear the sad calling of the crows. Resigned as I am, I wonder which generation will put an end to war. The bitterness of my life's journey has no match."

1603

The Valley of 10,000 Waterfalls

A gorge formed by two cliffs:
at the floor, one hundred streams flow.
Springs gurgle throughout the day—
across the way and near at hand
water drizzles.
Surprise at the steep, green-leafed cliffs:
two white dragons emerge—
looking closer, I see in the high cliff-cut sky
a rainbow
of 10,000 effervescent colors
plunging
to the valley floor.

Thunder roars through daylight;
stone pillars struck with wind—
pool after pool curves, spilling
into one another.
A fountainhead bubbles, overflows.
My heart unfurls in this magnificent scenery—
the Creator's grace deserves endless praise.
Xie Lingyun strolled Shimen,
Li Bai visited Lu Mountain;
a thousand years may pass,
but no land could surpass this beauty.

1603

Tosol Temple

Tosol is a renowned temple—
the Amitabha Buddha statue
causes all devils to surrender.

At the temple, an old monk
rests in comfort.

Worn out clothes hang on a mossy wall,
cold well water fills a porcelain jar.

I come to ask about Buddhism—
the old monk simply bows to me
uttering no word
hands clasped.

1603

Arriving at the County Office, I Climb to "Evolving Crane" Pavilion

The clerk leaves. The empty garden calms.
Climbing to the pavilion, I swell with emotion.
Mountains in all directions issue salutations—
the spirit of the stream bends naturally in gentle curves.

Evening birds sing their greetings to men—
chrysanthemums bloom, their intention fully exhausted.
Unchained, a strong wind blows through a field—
I forget all the duties of a magistrate.

1604

Indulgence

Fields and rice paddies, an abandoned desert.
Half the villagers, dead.
Taxes frequently collected,
a drought, a plague of insects.

In politics, it's impossible
to be the best disciple of Confucius;
I have compassion only for my hometown.
Vaguely, I feel shame from my salary:
2,000 bags of rice
and still not practicing virtuous governance.

1604

Lazy Old Man Visits

A guest comes with the east wind—
the change revives me from illness.
We dance like Xie Shang—
for ages, we've loved to drink.

He's still a painter,
but entrusts his life to wine jars.
This low official knows
the meaninglessness of things,
knows the value of returning
to ways of nature.

1605

On Being Passed Over for an Appointment to Hong County, Earned by Chamin

For years now, only writers
have been appointed to Hong County—
the poems of So and Chŏng
have won fame for their excellence.
This morning, the black-braided copper seal
goes to Chamin.
From the beginning, my tidy talent
was never good enough
for Hong County.

1607

Self Misery

Seoul, full of spring blushes—
the jesters' mirth has no end.
Drifting cattail seeds fill the streets—
my sleeves, moist with pink petals.

Sweet flute songs, elegant through the night—
gold jars of wine, still not empty at dawn.
Somehow I feel such sorrow from my illness—
I can only paint plums covered with snow.

1607

Falling Blossoms

I

Slanting wind perversely shakes cherry blossoms—
the murmuring breeze looses a red rain of petals.
People scatter after a lakeside spring party—
hairs from chignons and topknots flitter on a gold-threaded mat.

II

Mournful butterflies quietly shield fallen blossoms—
a small garden in meager sunlight tears at my heart.
As if the Eastern Emperor knew the spring's sadness,
wind turns the petals, like a dancer on a stage.

III

I grieve the florid pink tints, dried and falling
in my garden. These loose petals, like me,
would rather blow east and west
than be trapped by holly-green moss.

IV

The peach and plum trees boastfully compete for the richest,
most precious appearance, mocking solid but plain bamboo
and austere pines. In three quick months the rays of spring end—
only pine and bamboo keep their 10,000 shades of green.

V

All the leaves, fallen in wind, fluttering—one whirls
into a drawn curtain, another spoils a pond's surface.
Who knows when Heaven will bestow honor or disgrace?
There's no justice in whims of wind.

1607

First Feelings on Arriving at Samch'ok County

My late father was appointed to this county—
forty-five years have since passed.
I want to visit men who know my father's stories,
to walk where he once did,
but the traces have vanished.
What generations gave me, my inheritance,
I have shamefully made into failure.
A wall of ice
will never melt
into black scales.
Only by remembering family precepts
will one not fall—
how dare I presume fame
as great as the virtuous of history?

1607

Writing in My Study

Simple people are so easily governed. Who says a magistrate's job is wearisome? My "attention" bell rarely rings when judging disputes. I'm not ignorant, so my duties finish quickly.

The eastern annex is large and calm; on both sides, pears and persimmons grow. Lush shadows constantly undulate—through my window, a breeze blows. On a wide mat, I lean on a black recliner; it's so satisfying to let go of my tiredness.

Five wagons of books have trailed each journey of mine—I've always loved to read. Opening my chest, I've arranged the bookshelves, full; *reading is such a delight!*

The calligraphy of Han hangs near a north window, and a picture by Yi spreads over my east wall. The bones of these men already rot; considering their lives, I can only sigh.

I've waited six years for this, my one desire: to enjoy this pleasure as much as I like. Being sent to this place of ease suits me well. I don't dare forget the high grace of the King. What I worry about is governing fairly; I haven't extended enough kindness or favors. Savory dishes about my room, though fields and paddies fall into famine. These thoughts redden my face with shame. Though I do no work, I still collect my pay; I hope I can avoid the people's disgust.

Whoever the next magistrate is, I pray fate will not let him laugh at this writing.

1607

Upon Hearing of My Dismissal

I

I've long read about Buddhist practices—
my heart would rest nowhere else.
Like the Buddhist Zhou Yong,
I haven't abandoned my wife,
or like He, I don't worry
about avoiding meat.
My place is not that of a magistrate's—
how then can my dismissal
bring me sorrow?

Life follows the path of destiny—
in my dreams
I again long for the Buddha.

II

The rules of Confucius
never limited my freedom—
the movements of time
must be left to nature.

It's right for people to follow their own ways—
I will complete
the journey of my life.

Close friends offer consolation,
my wife and children grow discontented,
yet this news is so delightful,
as if something's been won—
like Li Bai and Du Fu
fortunately
I've earned some fame.

1607

71

An Improvised Poem

Shadowed summer landscape forms—
signs of rain distill to a weak chill.
Rightly so, this traveler is impressed,
but in such a strange town, I know no one.
The sky filled by a succulent moon—
a wave of mist floats on the sea.
Alone, I bear the sorrow of solitude—
my heart, wounded—
I lean on balustrades
empty.

1607

A Forest of Fragrant Flowers

Entering the valley, another mountain rises—
along a stream, the living scent of grass.
I stop at an old inn to rest from the saddle—
I rent a bed, and lay my head on a pillow.
Bird song I don't recognize quietly sounds;
deep in the forest, aromas of late afternoon
drift. This tired man has no time to rest—
his white hair's sorrow, from swells of time.

1607

Remorse

Too much slanderous speech overflows
consuming Heaven—
good or bad fortune
comes from men; I dare to escape.

I don't pray to the god of writing
for my exquisite children to die—
my family's history is one of poets
who write with phoenix quills.

All my life, I've respected
only Confucianists of old—
how can my cherished theories
resemble Taoism?

When questioned, I know
their hidden meaning.
Have I dared to disparage every Confucian saint?
Dare I beg my accusers to end their cunning?

1610

Waiting on Judgment in Prison, Regretting

Outside the prison gate, I wrap my clothes
put them away.

Imprisoned twice in a year
I chuckle at how often it's been.
Hell and Heaven, all one paradise—

why should I be ashamed
of the chains
binding my body?

1610

Recalling Happiness

The King's grace
is as great as the universe
above Earth.

By his order
I've returned my belt
of office.

Having no post
my body feels
carefree

declaring my dismissal
makes my heart
lazy.

My future plans
anchored in village fields,
my deep-rooted promise

reminds me of mountains
and the ocean.
An autumn wind

refreshes my mind—
whistling
I leave the gates of Seoul.

1610

Writing Sorrow II

My desire to retire from the King's postings extended over years—
who could know I would spend my elder days in exile?
Enemies slander as they please—
the pains of my heart, I share with a compassionate friend.

After spring, forest azaleas wash despair from my eyes—
after rain, mountain orioles call me from tranquil sleep.
Infusing tea weakens my diabetes—
where will I find the best stream water?

1611

Sending Away a Visitor, Sitting Alone

Piles of sutras, the warm stove, and unbroken silence—
my solitude, as an Immortal's house.
The warm day brightens plum blossoms, and my steps—
a light wind seeps through the gate, fells willow flowers.

I've given up writing. The roof-tile ink-stone slabs,
long dry. I should heat Dragon Tea over the strong fire.
Don't say I have no guests in this isolated place—
it's quite natural for bees of the mountain to visit.

1611

Ending a Collection

Through the years of my life
I've crafted poetry and calligraphy;
a thousand pieces of gold—
money spent yielding to my heart's desires.
Ten books of prose and poetry completed—
this old man will never write again.

1611

Endnotes

"*": All dates with an asterisk are speculative. Kyun lost the original poem in question during the war, but included the poem as he remembered it in his 1597 collection.

AFTER DU FU'S "OLD MEMORIES" POEMS
The sections of this poem have been interspersed in Part I of the manuscript to reflect the sequences of the war.

Part III, line 4 of the sections' sequence: Refers to "Shihao Officer," a poem by Du Fu which contains similar scenes.

AT THE REFUGEE CAMP
The title literally is, "At the Refugee Camp, I Write Eight Poems."

Section IV, line 1: The location refers to a border city (Uiju) where the King had retreated from the Japanese invasion.

Section VI, last line: The implication is that the governor is incompetent.

CLIMBING TO "WIDE VIEW" PAVILION
This poem was written on the way to China. All of Kyun's poems written in 1597 about traveling are on this thematic occasion. Kyun went as an emissary of the Korean government to ask China's help in repelling a second Japanese invasion.

DURING THE FULL MOON: A RESPONSE TO A POEM
Literally the title of the poem is, "During the Night of a Full Moon, an Envoy Showed Me Seven Poems in Short Form, Each Ending with a Word: 'Unparalleled,' 'Year,' 'Illumination,' 'Moon,' 'This,' 'Night,' 'Much.' I Write a Response." "Unparalleled" in section I is translated as "Matchless Pearl," while "Much" in section VII is translated as "shine"; this was done to increase fluidity of the poem.

Section 3, line 2: Heaven's Jade City, according to Taoism, is the capital of heaven.

ENDING A COLLECTION

Kyun edited his volumes of writing while in exile. During this time he wrote *Critical Realizations of an Old Man,* a book of criticism on poems dating from the Silla Dynasty to Kyun's contemporary moment.

FALLING BLOSSOMS

Sections II, III, and VI have been deleted as they relied too heavily on footnotes to be readily comprehensible to a general reader. The sequence remains intact. The deleted sections have been included here:

II

Fallen red fragrant petals waft, dot the earth—
an evening wind on my lacquered table.
Who knows the desolateness of a spring pavilion?
I feel like Queen Xu, regretting her half-made face.

III

Crisp wind and frigid rain blow heavily in late spring—
white petals drift, like smoke, saddening silk-clad women.
In the same way, Samlang went west to Shu,
while a jade face withered and fell on Mawei Hill.

VI

Bountiful blushed petals fall haphazard—a perfume of dust—
the heartlessness of wind and rain send off spring.
Unlike the story of Han Gao Pavilion and the women's jewels,
my garden is the Gold Valley where a beauty fell from a pavilion.

Section II: Queen Xu (Zhao Pei) was the wife of Yuan (507–554), an emperor of the Liang Dynasty who could only see out of one eye. As a joke, the queen made up half her face. When she greeted him, the emperor did not like the joke and left her.

Section III: Falling flowers are a symbol of prosperity ending. Women, often compared to flowers, here mourn their lost youth through the image of the falling petals.

Samlang was the childhood name of Xuan (685–762), an emperor of the Tang Dynasty. When he fled west from his palace because of a rebellion, his concubine, Lady Yang, died on Mawei Hill.

Section IV, line 3: Bamboo and pine trees in Korea traditionally represent pristine scholar-gentlemen because they are green (unchanging) year-round.

Section VI: In the Zhou Dynasty, Zheng Jiaofu met two ladies under Han Gao Pavilion. He said, "I'd like to have your jewelry," which they then gave. Jiaofu put the jewels in his breast pocket, but both the women and the jewels disappeared afer he walked ten steps. Kyun means to emphasize they were not real and their gifts were illusionary.

In the Jin Dynasty, Yuanzhu, a concubine, leapt to her death under Qingliang Pavilion in Gold Valley Garden. Why she jumped is unknown as of this writing. Kyun's intention is to emphasize that she was a real woman and her sudden death paralleled the end of spring.

FIRST FEELINGS ON ARRIVING AT SAMCH'ŎK COUNTY
Kyun was appointed magistrate to Samch'ŏk County. Within his first month of office he was dismissed.

Line 7: Refers to failure in courtly politics.

JULY 7th, EVENING, RECITING A MOURNFUL POEM
According to Korean legend, Vega and Altair, two lovers, meet and separate on this night. Rain on this night is said to be their tears.

LAMENTING THE SELF
Stanza 1, line 1: The Board of Rites was one of six boards under the Prime Minister; it had no political power.

Stanza 2, last line: Kyun wanted to fulfill his ambitions before retiring from the world; here, he transfers that decision onto the Queen of Heaven, a ruler of Taoist Immortals.

Stanza 3, last line: This water was said to have low buoyancy—nothing could float on it. To get to heaven, one first had to "climb the ladder" then "cross the water."

THE LONGING OF HWANG COUNTY WOMEN
Section VI, line 2: Literally refers to the pattern on the silk; figuratively, a man enjoying many women.

ON BEING PASSED OVER FOR AN APPOINTMENT TO HONG COUNTY
Line 3: So, Se-yang and Chŏng, Sa-ryong were the most famous among the officials of Hong County for their poems.

OVER-NIGHTING IN A COUNTRY HOUSE
The title more literally is "Over-nighting in a Tŏgwŏn House"; Tŏgwŏn is the name of a village in the deep country of Korea's Hamgyŏng Province.

Section I, last line: In the time of the Japanese invasions, Korea was able finally to expel the Japanese in large part by controlling the sea lanes.

Section II, stanza 4, line 1: Literally "six fantastic stratagems," a plan to defeat the enemy without great suffering to common people.

POEMS IN SHORT FORM
Section I, line 1: Snow Pear House was the name of a house in Kangnŭng owned by the brother of Kyun's grandfather-in-law.

Section III, last line: When Li Bai was young, he dreamed of a brush that turned into a flower. In the following days he became a celebrated poet.

Section IV, stanza 3, line 2: The West River Poets were poets of a famous Song Dynasty style.

SAYING GOODBYE TO RYU, YŎN-SUK
Stanza 1, lines 4 and 5: A cither is a musical instrument somewhat similar to the dulcimer, while a kist is a small chest, often used for storing books.

SELF MISERY
Stanza 2, last line: Plums are a fruit known for struggling in winter but still blossoming in snow.

SHARING POEMS
Four poets—Kyun, Yi Tal, Chŏng, Si-mang and Yun, O-jŏng—each took a Chinese character ("snow," "covered," "mountain," "range") and made a poem. Kyun's character was "mountain," thus this poem in Chinese ends with that character. Kyun had recently been impeached and was in seclusion on a mountain.

Stanza 1, line 6: Hats worn by simple country scholars who had no official government post.

TOSOL TEMPLE
"Tosol" is the fourth of six heavens where Matreiya Boddhisattva is said to live.

UPON ARRIVAL IN KANGNŬNG
Stanza 1, line 2: 1,000 li is approximately 400 km.

UPON HEARING OF MY DISMISSAL
According to *The Analects of Qi*, both Zhou Yong and He Yin were practitioners of Buddhism. The King once asked Zhou Yong who was the better practitioner, Zhou Yong or He Yin. Zhou answered, "We are both simple practitioners. I didn't leave my wife, and He Yin didn't stop eating meat." In truth, both were humble and good practitioners who lived in the mountains; it is also true that Zhou never left his wife and He never stopped eating meat.

VISITING KING GUAN'S TOMB IN NORTHERN CHINA
Last stanza: The image of a crying cuckoo and reddened flowers combine in Asian culture to indicate intense sadness.

WRITING IN MY STUDY
This poem was written during the thirteen day period of Kyun's appointment to Samch'ŏk County.

Line 8: "Han" refers to Han, Sŏk-pong (1543-1605), while "Yi" refers to the painter Yi Chŏng (1578-1607). Both were Kyun's friends.

WRITTEN ON THE FERRY
Last line: "Missteps" refers to Kyun's well-known anti-social, outspoken, and unmannered way of speaking. It was unusual in Kyun's day to be sent abroad twice in a year as an envoy.

Appendix 1: Lands and Locations

Beili: Literally "North Village," a phrase that could act both literally and as an idiom for a place, usually in a city, where wine and courtesans could be found.

Blue Mountain: A place of paradise imagined by Kyun.

Changan: The capital city of China during the Tang Dynasty.

Changnŭng: A district in Seoul.

Chengdu: A city in China, the old capital of Shu in the Three Kingdoms era.

Ch'ŏrwŏn Castle: Ch'ŏrwŏn is a town in South Korea's Kangwŏn Province near the border of present day North Korea.

Diamond Mountains: Located in Kangwŏn Province, the mountains from this range pass through present day North and South Korea.

Hong County: A county in Korea's Ch'ungch'ŏng Province.

Hongnong: A small town of antiquity in Chŏlla Province which was an artist's colony.

Hwang County: A county of China that borders present day North Korea.

Iron Mountain River: The Imjin River. If one is traveling north from Seoul, he or she must cross the river. Doing so is nuanced with a feeling of leaving Korea.

The Island of Immortals (Penglai Island): Mountain spirits (Taoist Immortals) were said to live on the Island of Immortals, an island in the middle of the Po Sea.

Lu Mountain: Lu Mountain is east of Changan. Xuanzong (685-762), a Tang

Emperor, built a special palace there for his concubine, Lady Yang. The location is famous for waterfalls and hot springs; to visit the waterfall one has to descend 1,200 steps.

The Mountain of Immortals (Penglai Mountain): The specific mountain home of many heavenly Immortals on the Island of Immortals.

Peaceful River: The Yalu River on the border shared by China and present day North Korea.

Po Sea: A "magical" sea between Korea and China reputedly on the western side of the Korean peninsula.

Samch'ŏk County: A county on the eastern coastline of Korea, just south of Kangnŭng.

Shimen: Located in Xanxi Province where the young Li Bai once lived. Literally, "Shimen" means "Stone Gate," though as an idiom, it suggests a deep country location to live as a hermit.

Tanyang: A county and city in Ch'ungch'ŏng Province.

The Valley of 10,000 Waterfalls: A valley within the Diamond Mountains in Korea.

West Castle's river border: The location refers to a border city (Uiju) where the King had retreated from the Japanese invasion.

Appendix 2: Reference for Important Names

Anren: The penname of Pan Yue (247-300), a handsome, "brilliant," Jin poet who became arrogantly conceited after earning a high position by flattering officials. He is considered the most handsome man in Chinese history. He is especially remembered for his three-poem series on his wife's death, the first poem being titled, "Mourning My Wife." He believed poems and paintings should be spontaneously and fluidly created, like running water, while at the same time rooted in an objective rendering of emotions.

Chamin: The Confucian given name ("penname") of Yi, An-nul (1571-1637), a close friend of Kyun's.

Chŏng, Sa-ryong: (1491-1570, penname Hoŭm) was a Minister three times and an official poet of the Korean government.

Chŏng, Si-mang: Chŏng, Si-mang (1586-?) earned the highest score on government exams for civil service, and was the governor of a province.

Dongpo: Su Dongpo (1036-1101) had many talents, including calligraphy and painting.

Du Fu: A Tang poet troubled by war.

The Eastern Emperor: In Taoism, the Eastern Emperor of mountains spirits is also the Creator.

General Suiyang: Literally, "a Governor of Suiyang," who possibly was Zhang Xun. In Chinese custom, the defender of a place assumed the name of that place, so that "Governor of Suiyang" becomes "Governor Suiyang." The translation goes one step further by making "Governor" into "General," the duty assumed by the Governor.

General Tiahou: Refers to Zhou Yafu, a General of Weidi in the Han Dynasty.

He Xun: He Xun (?-517) wrote his first poem at the age of eight; by twenty he was well-known, famous for writing poems on the theme of parting. Particularly good at poems in short form, He Xun was an influence on Du Fu.

Kim, Chong-chik: Kim, Chong-chik wrote against a somewhat illegitimate transfer of the royal lineage that took place in 1453. His body was exhumed and beheaded in 1499 during a purge of Confucian scholars.

King Guan: A renowned scholar-general remembered for his wisdom, Guan Yunzhang was posthumously made King under the first Emperor of the Han Dynasty.

Lazy Old Man: "Lazy Old Man" was the "art" (pen) name of Yi Chŏng (1578-1607), a celebrated painter.

Liu Zhangqing: A Tang poet remembered for his poems in the form of lines with five Chinese characters each, translated in this book as "short form."

Pan Yue: See Anren, above.

Ryu, Yŏn-suk: Who Ryu, Yŏn-suk was remains unknown as of this writing.

So, Se-yang: So, Se-yang (1486-1562) was a Deputy Prime Minister. Besides poetry, he is also remembered for his calligraphy.

Wang Can: A poet who lived during the Three Kingdoms period in China, Wang Can was often involved in and conflicted by war.

White Monkey: Who or what the White Monkey was is unknown as of this writing.

Xiangru: A Han Dynasty poet, Xima Xiangru was known as a calm personality.

Xie Lingyun: Xie Lingyun (385-483) was one of the most famous landscape poets in China.

Xie Shang: A governor in the Jin Dynasty who presided over several remarkable government achievements. Xie Shang was reputedly a musical genius.

Yellow Stone: Refers to a story in which Zhang Liang (?-168 BCE), an exceptional tactician, became a yellow stone on Gucheng Mountain.

Yin Keng: Yin Keng (?-?) wrote landscape poetry and was an influence on Du Fu.

Yun, O-jŏng: Who Yun, O-jŏng was remains unknown as of this writing.

Zhang Xun: Zhang Xun (?-757) was a general of the Tang Dynasty who led armies against rebellions. He was also a magistrate of Suiyang.

Zhuge Liang: An exceptional tactician and Prime Minister of the western Han Dynasty's first Emperor (181-234); he helped Sun Quan, King of Wu, at the Battle of Red Cliff in 208.

Zi Xia: Zi Xia (250-305) was a poet who wrote a famous book-length poem titled "The Three Capitals" about the three kingdoms of ancient China. The poem was written over a period of ten years and consisted of 10,000 characters.

Zuo Si: A poet of the Jin Dynasty who was an influence on Li Bai. He is also remembered for writing historically-themed poems.

Appendix 3: Excerpts
from Hŏ Kyun Manuscript Discovered in 2006

Resting at a Water Station

Down from the pass—the path, slippery,
the steep hills, endless.
Winter's early cold freezes my hands and feet—
people and horses slip on the ice, fall flat on the ground.

The narrow road twists, ascends between coarse stone walls—
clouds fill the sky at a high pass.
Before us, pure river waters—
I want to cross, but alas, there's no bridge or boat.

Riding a wagon, I ford the mountain river—
the deep water envelops my wagon to its hub.
Ahead, three thousand li of the Emperor's land—
how wide and long is the Lao Wilderness?

I travel only for the King's urgent work—
in this land, I endure frost and rain.
An old fortress covered by withered grass—
a watchman's horn signals a forlorn sunset.

I remember my home's gardens in the extreme distance—
tears fall, moistening my cape and coat.

1615

Using a Rhyme by Yuanming, a Scholar of the Empire's East

In Korea, there was a scholar,
who, though thin, had a fully developed mind.
Sometimes he met travelers who visited—
though an official, his clothes and hat were humble.
He lived among rocks and stones of a cave,
but his hair and face remained youthful.
He made no trouble for his wife or children,
faithfully accepting neither fame nor profit.
He only sat and watched white clouds,
the way edges of a thousand peaks
appeared and disappeared behind them.
There, wind and streams gushed, rippling into music—
it was not necessary to play a lute.

It's difficult to make a proud life—
in the red of evening, phoenixes and peacocks fly.
I've given great effort, such as the elderly claim—
this I swear: like Yuanming, my fires will never grow cold.

1616

Tao Yuanming (365–427) was a Chinese poet who, after becoming a magistrate, retired and returned home after only eighty days of service.

Passing the Mountain of Falcons and Pines

At Dragon Bay, the green mountains of this range seem to doze—
I sit, facing the mountains; I am a guest of these hosts.
Over 10,000 li, I've come again to these mountains—
they are like hometown friends who've never changed.

Spring mud wrinkles the road; our horses tred with difficulty—
this seasoned traveler hastens to return, has not a moment to relax.
March has nearly ended, and flowers begin to bloom—
nearby, evening wind blows rain.

1616

The Mountain of Falcons and Pines is near the border Korea shares with China.

Dragon Bay is a bay at the ferry crossing estuary of the Yalu River between Korea and China.

Bibliography

The Academy of Korean Studies. *A Chronological Table of Korean History.* Seoul: Tongbang Media. 2004.

——. *Dictionary of Korean-Chinese Characters.* Seoul: Tan'guk University Press. 2002.

——. *Encyclopedia of Korean Culture.* Seoul: Tongbang Media. 2004.

Choe-Wall, Yang Hi. *Vision of a Phoenix.* New York: Cornell University Press. 2003.

Choe, Wolhee and Constantine Contogenis, trans. *Songs of the Kisaeng.* Rochester, NY: BOA Editions, Ltd. 1997.

Chŏn, Song-yŏl. *A Study on Poems of the Early Yi Dynasty.* Seoul: Ihoe. 2001.

Chi, Se-hwa. *A History of Chinese Culture.* Seoul: Ilbit. 2002.

Ha, Kyŏng-jin and T'ae-wŏn Ki. *Commentary on Korean Poems.* Seoul: Asia Munhwasa. 1995.

Hinton, David, trans. *The Selected Poems of Li Po.* New York: New Directions. 1996.

Hŏ, Kyŏng-jin. *A Biography of Hŏ Kyun.* Seoul: Tolbege. 2002.

Hŏ, Kyŏng-jin, ed. *The Collected Poems of Nansŏrhŏn.* Seoul: P'yŏngminsa. 1999.

——. *The Selected Poems of Hŏ Pong.* Seoul: Pyŏngminsa. 1996.

——. *The Selected Poems of Hŏ Kyun.* Seoul: Pyŏngminsa. 1996.

——. *The Selected Poems of Yi Tal.* Seoul: Pyŏngminsa. 1996.

Hŏ, Kyun. *Criticism.* Ed. by Kyŏng-jin Hŏ. Seoul: Minŏmsa. 1982.

Hŏ, Mi-ja. *A Study on Hŏ, Nansŏrhŏn.* Seoul: Sŏngsin University Press. 1984.

Hong, Sang-hun. *The Collected Poems of Li He.* Seoul: Myŏngmundang. 2007.

Kim, Chang-hwan, and Pang Yi. *Tai Ping Guangji.* Seoul: Hakgobang. 2004.

Kim, Chi-yŏng. *The World of Poems by Korean Poetesses.* Seoul: Yŏgang. 2002.

Kim, Myung-hee. *The Literature of Hŏ, Nansŏrhŏn.* Seoul: Jibmoongdang. 1987.

Kim, Sŏn. *Hŏ Kyun, A Thunder.* Seoul: Yemundang. 2000.

Kim, Sŏng-nam. *Hŏ, Nansŏrhŏn.* Seoul: Tongmunsŏn. 2003.

——. *A Study on the Poems of Hŏ, Nansŏrhŏn.* Seoul: Somyŏng. 2002.

Kim-Shin, Myŏng-suk. *Hŏ, Nansŏrhŏn, A Novel.* Seoul: Gŭmto. 1999.

Kubo, Noritada. *Gods and Spirits of Taoism.* Seoul: Ppuriwaipari. 2002.

Kwon, Kyŏgsam. *Commentary on Poems by Koreans.* Seoul: Taunsa. 2003.

Li, Bai. *Yuefu Poems.* Trans. by Ok-kyŏng Chin. Seoul: Saram Gwa Chaek. 1998.

Mun, Kyŏng-hyŏn, trans. *The Collected Poems of Nansŏrhŏn.* Seoul: Boryŏngak. 1972.

Nakai, Kenji. *The Words of Poems by Hŏ, Nansŏrhŏn.* Trans. by Mi-ja Hŏ. Seoul: Kukhakcharyowŏn. 2003.

O, Hae-in, trans. *The Poems of Nansŏrhŏn.* Seoul: Haein. 1980.

Owen, Stephen. *The Poetry of the Early Tang.* Trans. by Sae-hu Chang. Seoul: Joongmoon. 2000.

——. *The High Tang.* Cambridge: Yale University Press. *1981.*

——. *The Late Tang.* Boston: Harvard University Asia Center. 2006.

Pak, Sam-su, trans. *Poems of Wang Wei.* Seoul: Sekyesa. 1993.

Pak, Yŏng-ho. *The Literature and Taoism of Hŏ Kyun.* Seoul: Taehaksa. 1999.

Pak, Yŏng-kyu. *The Eunuch and the Palace Maid.* Seoul: Kimyŏngsa. 2004.

Paludau, Ann. *A Chronicle of Chinese Emperors.* Trans. by Tong-chin Yi. Seoul: Kangin Gongbang. 2004.

Qu, Yuan. *Chuci.* Trans. by Minsu Yi. Seoul: Myŏngmundang. 1992.

Rexroth, Kenneth, and Ling Chung, trans. *Women Poets of China.* New York: New Directions. 1972.

Ryu, Wie. *Chinese Civilization in a New Light.* Trans. by Yang-su Kim. Seoul: Sigongsa. 2001.

Shan, Han. *Cold Mountain.* Trans. by Burton Watson. New York: Columbia University Press. 1970.

Shin, Myŏng-ho. *Palace Maid.* Seoul: Sigongsa. 2004.

——. *The Culture of the Palace.* Seoul: Tolbege. 2002.

The Special Committee for Creating a Chinese-Korean Dictionary. *Chinese-Korean Dictionary.* Seoul: Kyohaksa. 2004.

The Special Committee for Creating a Dictionary of Chinese Particles. *Dictionary of Chinese Particles.* Seoul: Hyŏnmasa. 2003.

The Special Committee for Creating a Dictionary of Korean History. *Dictionary of Korean History.* Seoul: Kyohaksa. 1985.

The Special Committee for Creating a Korean-English Dictionary of Culture and Language. *Korean-English Dictionary of Culture and Language.* Seoul: Hansebin. 2003.

Tamagi, Ogawa. *An Introduction to Poems of the Tang.* Trans. by Kyŏng-ho Sim. Seoul: Ihoe. 1998.

Wagner, Edward W. *A New History of Korea.* Seoul: Ilchokak. 1984.

Yi, Ik. *A Book of Poems with Comments.* Trans. by Suk-ki Choe. Seoul: Wahwu 1996.

Yi, Song-mi. *Fragrance, Elegance, and Virtue.* Seoul: Daewonsa. 2002.

Yi, Yŏng-ju, trans. *Translations of the Early Poems of Du Fu.* Seoul: Sol. 1999.

The Translators

Ian Haight was the co-organizer and translator for the UN's global poetry readings held annually in Pusan, Korea from 2002-4. He has been awarded translation grants from the Daesan Foundation, Korea Literary Translation Institute, and Baroboin Buddhist Foundation. In 2003, he was cited for translation excellence by the KLTI. For more information, please visit ianhaight.com.

T'ae-yŏng Hŏ has been awarded several translation grants from the Daesan Foundation and Korea Literary Translation Institute. Working from the original classical Chinese, his translations of Korean poetry have appeared in *Runes, New Orleans Review,* and *Atlanta Review.*

The Korean Voices Series

Scale and Stairs
Selected Poems of Heeduk Ra
Translated by Won-chung Kim and Christopher Merrill
Volume 14   978-1-893996-24-3   88 pages $17.00

One Human Family & Other Stories — Chung Yeun-hee
Translated by Hyun-jae Yee Sallee
Volume 13   978-1-893996-87-8   232 pages $16.00

Woman on the Terrace — Poems by Moon Chung-hee
Translated by Seong-kon Kim and Alec Gordon
Volume 12   978-1-87399686-1   120 pages $18.00

Eyes of Dew — Poems by Chonggi Mah
Translated by Brother Anthony of Taizé
Volume 11   1-893996-79-4$ 160 pages   16.00

Even Birds Leave the World — Selected Poems of Ji-woo Hwang
Translated by Won-chun Kim & Christopher Merrill
Volume 10   1-893996-45-x   104 pages $14.00

The Depths of a Clam — Selected Poems of Kim Kwang-kyu
Translated by Brother Anthony of Taize
Volume 9   1-893996-43-3   160 pages $16.00

Echoing Song: Contemporary Korean Women Poets
Edited by Peter H. Lee
Volume 8   1-893996-35-2   304 pages $18.00

Among the Flowering Reeds: Classic Korean Poems in Chinese
Edited and translated by Kim Jong-gil
Volume 7   1-893996-54-9   152 pages $16.00

Brother Enemy: Poems of the Korean War
Edited and translated by Suh Ji-moon
Volume 6   1-893996-20-4   *176 pages*   *$16.00*

Shrapnel and Other Stories — Selected Stories of Dong-ha Lee
Translated by Hyun-jae Yee Sallee
Volume 5   1-893996-53-0   *176 pages*   *$16.00*

Strong Wind At Mishi Pass   — Poems by Tong-gyu Hwang
Translated by Seong-kon Kim & Dennis Maloney
Volume 4   1-893996-10-7   *118 pages*   *$15.00*

A Sketch of the Fading Sun — Stories of Wan-suh Park
Translated by Hyun-jae Yee Sallee
Volume 3   1-877727-93-8   *200 pages*   *$15.00*

Heart's Agony: Selected Poems of Chiha Kim
Translated by Won-chun Kim and James Han
Volume 2   1-877727-84-9   *128 pages*   *$14.00 paper*

The Snowy Road: An Anthology of Korean Fiction
Translated by Hyun-jae Yee Sallee
Volume 1   1-877727-19-9   *168 pages*   *$12.00 paper*